Blurtso goes around

and comes around

by Alan Davison

Shield Publishers

ISBN-13: 978-0966144130
ISBN-10: 0966144139

Ahhh, the first snap of autumn,
co-eds on the Common, professors in the halls,
coffee in the cups, bulletins on the walls,
… and animals preparing for winter..

What are you taking this semester? said Alex. I'm taking a class called, "Nature or Nurture," said Blurtso. Of course, said Alex, the debate over the effect of heredity versus environment on personal development. Really? said Blurtso, I thought it was a spelling class.

I wonder, said Pablo,
if there are donkeys on other planets.

The leaves are changing. The world is a year older and I'm a year older. But for those born this past year, the world is brand new. If you've been here a while it's hard to see the world as brand new. You see things that aren't what they used to be and become nostalgic for the way they used to be. Or maybe you just become nostalgic for the way you used to see things, when you used to see things as brand new.

An individual blade of grass is inconceivable. It only exists as the pattern of relationships—seed, soil, roots, water, sun—called grass. An individual donkey is also inconceivable.

If a single blade of grass exists only as a part of the pattern called grass, and the pattern called grass exists only as a part of the pattern called the world, and the pattern called the world exists only as a part of the pattern called the universe, then everything that exists exists only as pattern, and it is impossible to speak of grass, or pumpkin pies, or "Blurtso", without speaking of the universe.

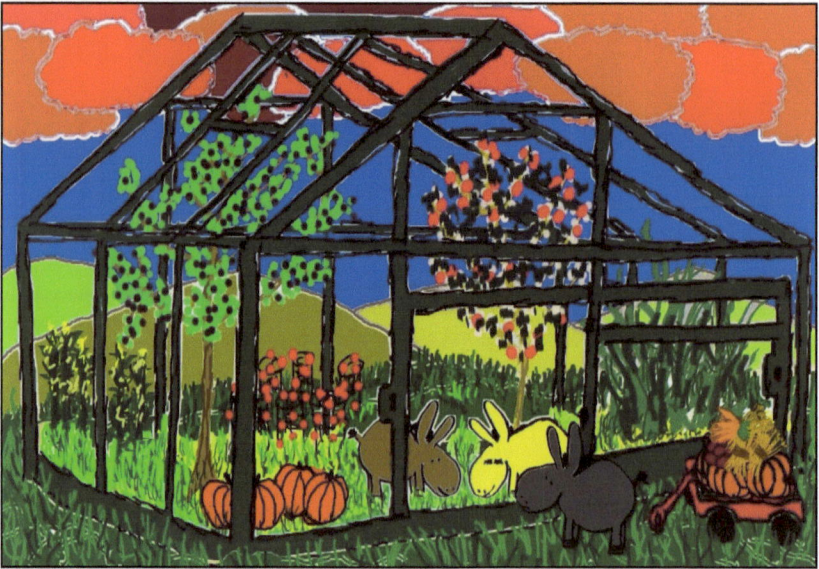

Hello, said Pablo and Bonny. Hello, said Blurtso.
What are you doing? We're taking veggies to our
cabin, said Pablo. How about you? I'm going to
class, said Blurtso. Really? said Bonny. Why don't
you come visit when you're done? Ditto would love
to see you. Ditto? said Blurtso. Ditto is Bonny's
stuffed animal, said Pablo. Oh, said Blurtso. But he's
remarkably intelligent, said Bonny. I'm sure he is,
said Blurtso. So you'll come? said Bonny. I don't
think so, said Blurtso, I've got an exam tomorrow.
That's too bad, said Pablo, we could go for a swim.
With the ducks? said Blurtso. Of course, said Pablo.
Hmm, said Blurtso, do you know anything about the
underlying causes of World War One? No, said
Pablo, but I'm sure we can figure it out. Great! said
Blurtso. I'll see you after class.

No one's home... except Bonny's stuffed animal.
He sure is funny-looking.
Rabbit-sized ears, boxing-
glove nose, two eyes that
may as well be one. I wonder
what he's supposed to be?
His hooves are wrong for a
rabbit... and his nose is wrong for a rhino... maybe
he's a camel or a mouse... or an overstuffed rat... I
wonder if he can swim... maybe he's a sea creature
who's stranded on land... or a land creature who
yearns for the sea... Hah! He sure looks funny! But
even so... he's really quite handsome.

So, said Blurtso, WWI was the result of a series of
diplomatic clashes over European and colonial
issues that stemmed from the changing balance of
power after 1867? Exactly, said Pablo.

Wow, said Blurtso, the corn in Pablo's garden has really grown. I wonder how far it goes? I wonder if it goes all the way to Nebraska? I've never been to Nebraska, but I've seen a lot of corn. The people in Nebraska must be happy with their corn.

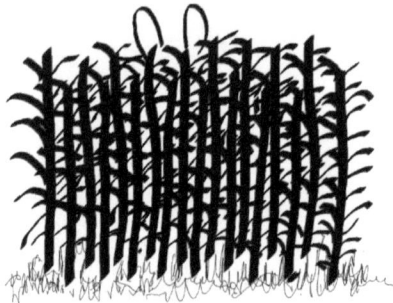

I wonder if I should move to Nebraska? I wonder how many cornfields it is from here to Nebraska? Maybe it's many cornfields away or maybe it's just one big cornfield. I would be very happy if it's only a cornfield away. I can hardly wait to get to Nebraska. This corn is very tall. Only a giraffe could see over this corn. I wonder if there are many giraffes in Nebraska. I hope so. I would love to see a cornfield full of giraffes. And penguins. I would

8

love to see a cornfield full of giraffes and penguins and maybe even a pterodactyl. Wouldn't that be something, giraffes, penguins, and pterodactyls. I can hardly wait to get to Nebraska. Wow, I've been walking a long time. Nebraska is farther than I thought. I wonder if I'm getting close? I wonder if I already passed it? I wonder if I passed it and am now walking away? I wish I could see above the corn. I haven't found a single giraffe.

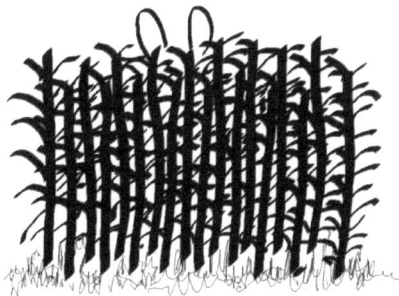

I think I'm walking in circles. I wonder if I'm walking in big circles or little circles? If I walk in bigger and bigger circles I should reach the edge of the field. I wonder what's beyond the cornfield? I wonder if it's a canefield? A canefield is taller than a cornfield. Even a giraffe wouldn't walk into a canefield. A giraffe wouldn't walk into a canefield or a cornfield, apparently. I should have turned back when I didn't see the giraffes. Yes, that's what I should have done, I should have followed the giraffes. Hey, what's this? An opening in the corn! Oh boy! I can hardly wait to see what's there! Hmmm, said Blurtso, would you look at that, a wide flat space. An empty space, without a single giraffe. That's not good. I wonder what's beyond this empty space? Probably another field. Blurtso looked at the field from which he had emerged, then he looked at the space. I guess if I walk along the edge of the corn I will get to where I went in. I wonder what time it is? The shadows of the corn are as long as my nose, so it must be before noon. Did I enter from the east or from the west? I think the east. Let's see, if the time is before noon and my shadow is to the right, I must be walking south. Maybe the entrance is to the south. Unless I'm walking away from the entrance…

And so he went, walking and worrying, figuring and fretting, gladdening and saddening, until he eventually reached the entrance to the corn. The entrance! he said. Or is this the exit? Just then, Blurtso heard a rustle in the corn. What's that?! A giraffe! A penguin! A pterodactyl! Oh my good-ness! An enormous boxing-glove nose! Hello, said Pablo, emerging from the corn. A happier donkey at the entrance of a cornfield the world has never

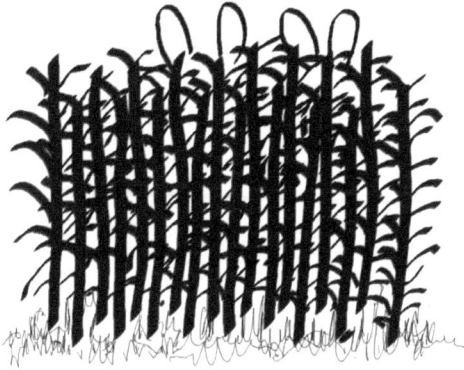

seen. How did you find the entrance? said Blurtso. Simple, said Pablo, I followed the giraffes. Did you see any pterodactyls? said Blurtso. Of course not, said Pablo, Nebraska is only six thousand years old.

Ooops, said Blurtso, stumbling on a hole in the grass. I almost turned my hoof and fell. I never do that. At least I didn't used to. I guess in the future I'll stumble more often. And then I'll fall. And one day I'll fall without stumbling. And then I won't get up, and I'll dream of the days when I could stumble and fall.

The moon is full. They say a full moon brings out the animal in you. I wonder what animal is in me? A bull, or a goat, or a parakeet? I've never really thought about my inner parakeet. I wonder how long it's been trying to get out? I wonder if it's unhealthy to keep it locked up. The world might be a different place, if we all got in touch with our inner parakeets.

What's your inner parakeet telling you? said Harlan. He's telling me, said Blurtso, that there's a half-eaten pumpkin pie in the fridge. What's yours telling you? He's telling me, said Harlan, that someone already finished the second half.

Hunger is the bow, whipped cream the arrow,
and pumpkin pie the target
one sights unflinchingly.

You have not spoken of pumpkin pie.
I have not spoken of pumpkin pie.
This is the true pumpkin pie.

A donkey was pursued by two tigers,
one from in front, one from behind.
He also had a Chemistry exam the next day.
"Is there any more pumpkin pie?" said the donkey.

What are you looking at? said Harlan. There's a crack in one of the window panes, said Blurtso. Is there? said Harlan. Yes, said Blurtso, a hairline crack in the bottom-right corner of the left door. So there is, said Harlan. It makes you think about the rest of the glass, said Blurtso, and the other panes that are still intact. Glass is made of sand, said Harlan. Is it? said Blurtso. Yes, said Harlan, quartz sand that has been heated to over 4,000 degrees fahrenheit. Glass is often overlooked, said Blurtso, until it has a crack. Yes it is, said Harlan. Do you think it should be replaced? said Blurtso. I don't know, said Harlan. The windows are laminated, said Blurtso, so it probably won't spread. And we might miss the crack, said Harlan, when it's gone. Yes, said Blurtso, and lose our appreciation for the panes that are not cracked.

One way to experience a moment completely,
is to try as hard as you can
to experience a moment completely,
until you experience complete frustration.

They say dogs bark when they see a spirit, and
they can sense when a person has died. But I've
never seen a spirit, even when I was standing next
to a barking dog. I wonder what else I'm missing?

Hmm, the cars are trying to drive in this storm. They've got their lights on and their wipers slapping. It's eerie to drive in a storm like this. Especially if your radio is broken and all you can hear is the thump of the blades... the snow sure looks soft... I'll bet I could leap from this tree house and the snow would break my fall. I'll bet I could do a back flip and land without a sound. But no one would believe it... if I didn't make a sound. People don't put much stock in silence.

The snow is gathering on my nose. I guess it's snowing faster than my nose can melt. I wonder how high it will get? It's collecting even faster now. My nose must be getting cold. Soon the snow will blur my features, and I'll become a rounded version of myself. A more-rounded version. Then I'll become a swollen lump. Then even that will smoothe over, and vanish without a trace.

****

Hmm, more snow. This winter is really something. I think my coat is turning white. Pretty soon I'll begin to look like a polar bear… or a polar donkey. And on a day like today, I'd be invisible. I wonder what it would be like to be invisible, and not have anyone notice me? I suppose I could always stomp one someone's shoe… to make sure I'm alive.

****

It's very quiet. I can't even hear the cars in the street. I wonder how much it's snowing at Bonny and Pablo's cabin? I'll bet you could stray from the path and not even know. You'd have to make a new path, which wouldn't be a path, but only a trail of wandering. Hmm, it's very quiet. I wonder how much it's snowing at Bonny and Pablo's cabin?

17

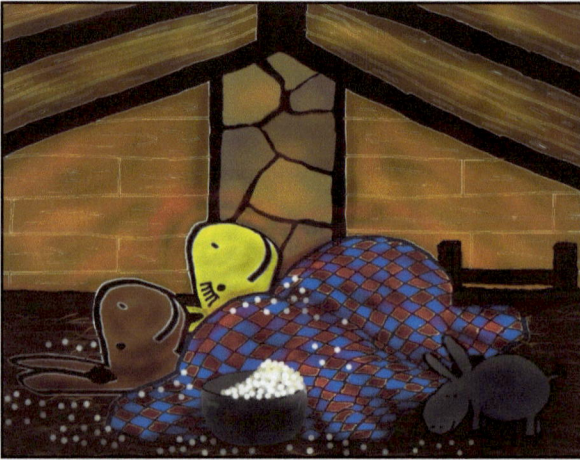

I love to watch the firelight, said Pablo. Yes, said Bonny, the reflection flickering on the ceiling, and the shadows shrinking and stretching. Do you think it's snowing? said Pablo. I hope so, said Bonny, Ditto loves the snow.

****

It must be midnight, thought Pablo, I can hear the last train. Today was a good day. A day of food, shelter, and company. I wonder what tomorrow will bring? Another day, I hope, of the same.

****

I can hear the outbound from Boston, thought Pablo. They say that everyone loves the sound of a train in the distance. I wonder why? Maybe it represents freedom, or adventure, or the romance of new people and places. Or maybe it just makes home and family seem that much sweeter.

Aging, said Bonny, is the growth of deterioration.

No, said Bonny, the stream never flows back.

There's nothing better than a blanket and cup of cocoa…watching next spring's lakes and streams drop from the sky.

The snow is light and fluffy today. Almost like the first snow of the season. Even in the middle of winter, the drudgery of old can be erased by the freshness of new.

I wonder if anyone will ever know all that's inside of me, and if I will know all that's inside of them? Or if that's impossible for creatures who are burdened with motion and words.

I don't think I've ever seen so much snow. There's no use trying to go anywhere. Or trying to do anything. It's like a day that fell through the calendar, a day without a number. Perfect for a book and a blanket, and another cup of cocoa.

I wonder what people did in New England before
television and Facebook? I guess they read books
to pass the winter hours… or wrote letters…
or practiced the piano…

. . . .

Hmm, thought Blurtso, the ants have returned to
the barn. I wonder what they do in winter… I've
never seen a colony migrating south. Maybe they
go deeper underground. They sure are in a hurry,
always going someplace. And as soon as they get
there, they go someplace else. They're almost
human… I wonder if ants ever sleep? I wonder
what they dream of? I wonder if they dream of
going here and there and back again? I suppose if
you dream of what you do when you're awake, it's
like you've never been asleep… Ants don't take
many naps. I've never seen an ant napping under a
tree. Whenever I'm under a tree, the ants that are
there crawl all over me. I wouldn't mind napping
with an ant, but I'm not sure they're capable. The
ability to nap is an uncommon skill… I wonder if
ants worry about the environment? I wonder what

they think of global warming? If I were an ant I would want to do something, but they act like they don't even care. Maybe they don't take themselves as seriously as we do. Maybe for them this world is just a testing ground, and they'll all get their reward in heaven. I wonder what an ant has to do to get into heaven? I wonder what heaven is for an ant? Maybe it's a warm barn with plenty of food. That's what it is for me. And since a warm barn with plenty of food always has a number of ants, and usually a donkey or two, then I must be a part of their heaven and they must be a part of mine. Maybe heaven is not a place at all… maybe it's a relationship.

The more you look at ants, the more they look like water… flowing here, flowing there, encountering an obstruction, flowing around it, flowing over it, or carrying it with them as they flow along. And just like too much of anything, if there are too many, they carry away everything in sight, until there is nothing left for others, and nothing left for themselves.

That ant is going the wrong way. He's straying from the pack. I wonder if he's sick? I wonder if the others will bring him back? Or if he'll discover a new way to be an ant?

Oh, oh, said Blurtso, do you see that ant? Yes, said

Harlan. What are we going to do? said Blurtso. I
don't mind a single ant, said Harlan, but when
you're surrounded by hundreds or thousands, they
can become unpleasant. Yes, said Blurtso, like
humans. Do you think he'll tell his friends about the
loft? said Harlan. I don't know, said Blurtso, maybe
he's a hermit ant. A hermit ant? said Harlan. Yes,
said Blurtso, an ant who rejects the frenetic pace and
consumerism of contemporary ant society, and goes
off on his own to contemplate nature and his relationship to the cosmos. Or maybe, said Harlan, he's
a scout ant.

I guess, said Harlan, he wasn't a hermit ant. It's very
unsettling, said Blurtso, when someone invades
your home. Yes, said Harlan, you feel violated. What
if they don't leave? said Blurtso. We'll make them
leave, said Harlan. How? said Blurtso. We'll turn off
the solar heater and open the doors, said Harlan, so
they'll get cold and go back to their underground
nest. That's a great idea, said Blurtso.

It's nice to be home, said Blurtso, it's nice to see our hay again, and pie tins, and cocoa powder, and coffee mugs, and my painting easel and brushes, and complete collection of Patrick O'Brian novels, and "Mister Ed" dvds, and Tony Robbins tapes, and patchwork blanket, and phonograph player and 1970's LPs, and Cutco knife set, and autographed copy of *Leaves of Grass*, and French door windows, and step ladder to the loft. We've only been gone three days, said Harlan. I know, said Blurtso, but it seems like years.

It's late now and most everyone is home. Resting and reflecting on the day, what went right and what went wrong, what to look forward to and what to dread. Or they're filling their eyes and ears with electric sights and sounds, while their heart, alone beneath the surface, reflects on the day.

This is a very nice barn, thought Blurtso. The roof doesn't leak and there is plenty of hay. I can stand here all day if I want to. While the rest of the world runs frantically toward and away from things, I can stand here all day... I suppose we can put up with almost anything as long as we have a safe place to go...

Hmm, a ray of sunlight is streaking through a crack in the door. It's so bright it makes the rest of the barn seem dark, and makes it difficult to notice anything else. It's amazing how much you miss... when you only focus on one thing.

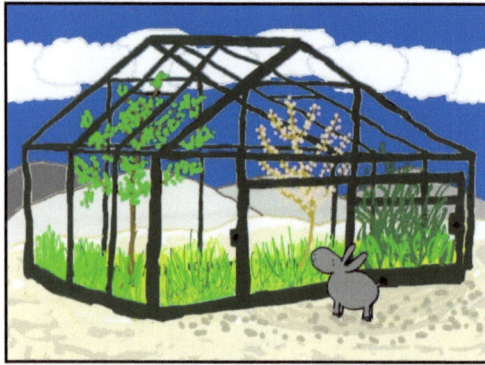

Hmm, thought Blurtso, since Pablo moved to his
cabin on Walden Pond his greenhouse is getting
out of control… I'd better do some grazing.

What are you doing? said Harlan. I'm grazing, said
Blurtso, I've got to get Pablo's greenhouse under
control. What about school? said Harlan. School
will have to wait, said Blurtso. O.k., said Harlan,
I'll take notes for you… is there anything you
need? No, said Blurtso, I have plenty to eat, and
the snow will quench my thirst. O.k., said Harlan,
I'll tell the professor why you're absent.

Hello, said the professor. Hello, said Blurtso. Your roommate told me why you missed class, said the professor. I'm sorry, said Blurtso, but this greenhouse is my responsibility. Your responsibility? said the professor. Yes, said Blurtso, it was entrusted to me, and I've neglected it too long. I admire your sense of duty, said the professor, but your grade will suffer. That's a price, said Blurtso, I'm prepared to pay. On the other hand, said the professor, you might be able to get service-learning credit. Service learning? said Blurtso. Yes, said the professor, for doing something that benefits the community. How, said Blurtso, does this benefit the community? Your greenhouse, said the professor, could be a model for self-sustainability in Cambridge. Really? said Blurtso. Yes, said the professor, but you'd have to be willing to talk to people about what you're doing and why you're doing it. I'm doing it, said Blurtso, because I waited too long, and I can't wait any longer. Exactly, said the professor.

Your greenhouse was all we talked about today in class, said Harlan. Really? said Blurtso. Yes, said Harlan, the professor gave us an article to read about Degrowth Theory. Degrowth theory? said Alex, isn't that an oxymoron? An oxymoron? said Blurtso. Yes, said Alex, a concept that is made up of contradictory or incongruous elements; growth implies increase, "de" implies the opposite, so you might as well say decrease. The professor explained that, said Harlan, he said the word implies the increase of communities choosing to decrease their consumption, a world where more people choose to live a simpler lifestyle. What does that have to do with my greenhouse? said Blurtso. Your greenhouse, said Harlan, is a self-sustaining environment, you could live forever in this green- house if you chose. Except, said Blurtso, for pumpkin pies. You could grow pumpkins, said Harlan. How would I cook them? You could use solar energy, said Alex. Isn't it hard to grow solar panels? said Blurtso. It's impossible, said Alex, but you could trade with others in the community, and eventually reduce the size of your environmental hoofprint. The goal is to be as self-sustaining as possible. My environmental hoofprint? said Blurtso, my hoofs aren't so big.

It sure is warm in here, said Harlan. It sure is, said Blurtso. That's because a greenhouse, said Alex, turns solar energy into thermal energy, which in turn creates a convection process. What? said Blurtso. Solar energy, said Alex, passes through the glass and gets absorbed by the ground and plants. The plants convert the sun's short wave infrared rays into long wave infrared rays—into heat energy—which can't escape the glass. Because the air is trapped, the warm air near the ground rises and the cool air near the ceiling falls, turning the greenhouse into a convection oven which forces the air to become warmer and warmer with each rise and fall. A convection oven? said Blurtso. Exactly, said Alex. Does that work on a small scale? said Blurtso. Of course it does, said Alex. So I could bake a pumpkin pie, said Blurtso, in a miniature greenhouse?

It's like a sauna today, said Harlan. Yes it is, said Blurtso. I'll bet it's unbearably hot in here in the summer, said Harlan. In the summer, said Blurtso, Pablo opens the door and the windows in the roof. Too bad, said Harlan, we can't do that with the earth. What? said Blurtso. You know, said Harlan, global warming and the greenhouse effect. What? said Blurtso. The heating of the earth's atmosphere due to fossil fuels and deforestation. Is that bad? said Blurtso. Disastrous, said Harlan. Why? said Blurtso. Because, said Harlan, it leads to extreme weather, rising sea levels, ocean acidification, and the extinction of species. The extinction of species? said Blurtso. Yes, said Harlan, penguins, seals, turtles, flamingos, salmon, clownfish, koala bears, polar bears, and eventually humans. Polar bears? said Blurtso. Yes, said Harlan. But I like polar bears, said Blurtso. So do I, said Harlan.

This is Suzy Starlight with Cambridge Community Television reporting live from the greenhouse at 2010 Clippety Clop Way, where the Harvard co-ed, Blurtso Lundif, is taking a stand for responsible living. Tell us if you would, Mr. Lundif, when did you first decide something had to be done? Last week, said Blurtso. And what is it you hope to do? I hope, said Blurtso, to graze on the grass that has grown amok, so that all plants can have their fair share of sun and sustenance. Their fair share? said Suzy. Yes, said Blurtso, and live in an environment of conscientious moderation. I see, said Suzy, and how long are you prepared to work towards that end? As long as it takes, said Blurtso. And you will remain in your greenhouse for the duration of the project? Yes, said Blurtso. How admirable, said Suzy, is there anything you would like to say to our viewing audience before we break away? Yes, said Blurtso. What is that? said Suzy. All donations to the project, said Blurtso, should be made in the form of small, medium, or large pumpkin pies.

Wow, said Harlan, the greenhouse looks great!
Yes, said Blurtso, there's nothing like having
friends. What will you do next? said Harlan. I'm
thinking, said Blurtso, of starting a Co-Op.

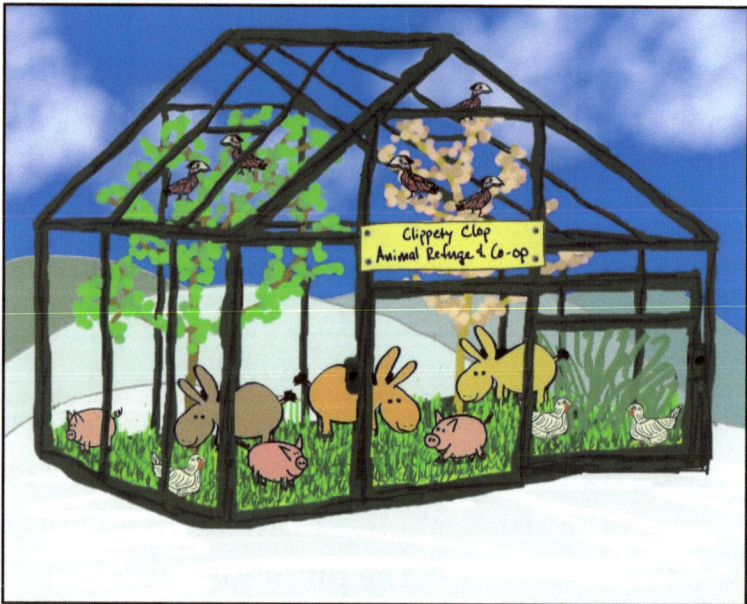

Clippety Clop
Animal Refuge & Co-op

Do you think we watch too much television? said
Blurtso. I don't know, said Harlan, I suppose it's
impossible to know if you're doing too much of
anything... until it's too late.

Hmm, thought Blurtso, would you look at that...
an abandoned tavern. A place where firelight once
flickered on the walls and ceiling, where animals
and people stopped for refreshment, exchanged
words and glances, and continued on their way.

I've opened and closed the latch on this barn door
every day for three years, said Blurtso, and I can't
remember what it looks like… I couldn't begin to
describe it, or describe a thousand other things I've
used again and again and again. Yes, said Harlan,
that's the way it is, we stumble blindly along, and
then one day we're gone and only the forgotten
things remain.

I saw that the animals from the Co-Op have moved
into the house, said Alex. Yes, said Blurtso, and
they think I'm some sort of guru.

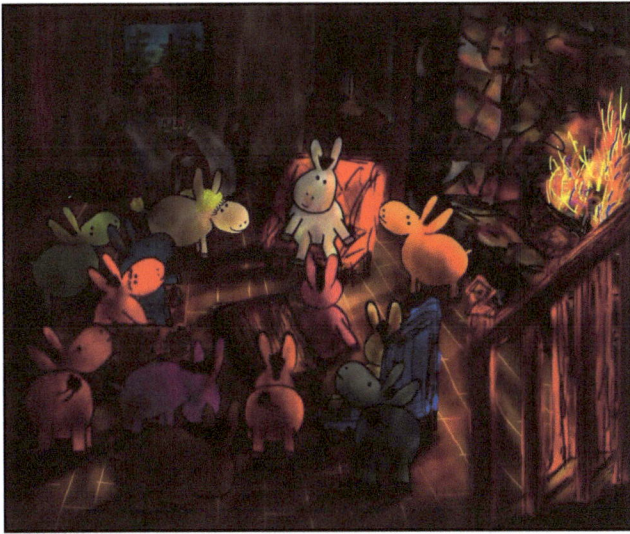

And they gathered before him and said,
"Teach us," and Blurtso replied,
"One who learns under another's teaching
to rise above another's teaching
is another's true teacher."

And they gathered before him and said, "Free us,"
and Blurtso replied, "You are free."
And they remained where they were, freely.

And they said, "What shall we do?"
and Blurtso replied:
"The river carves the bank,
and the bank reveals the river."

And they said, "Speak to us of rest,"
and Blurtso replied: "The wave travels many miles,
then breaks to pieces."

Can you teach me to do tai chi? said Blurtso.
Sure, said Harlan, we can begin with a simple
circling exercise.

More slowly, said Harlan, and a little less
like an airplane propeller.

I saw Blurtso yesterday, said Pablo, he told me he's
started a tai chi class in his barn.

Circle from side to side, said Blurtso,
shifting your weight from hoof to hoof...
left hoof full, right hoof empty,
right hoof full, left hoof empty,
see the pumpkin pie, see the empty pie tin...

I'm glad we're not moving into the house, said Blurtso. Why? said Harlan. Because, said Blurtso, I'm comfortable in the barn. So am I, said Harlan. I wonder, said Blurtso, if I underestimate the power of familiar things. Most people do, said Harlan. Do you think it keeps us from doing things we should do? Sometimes, said Harlan, it keeps us from following our heart. What do you mean? said Blurtso. To follow your heart you can't be chained to familiar things, you have to be open to change. Why? said Blurtso. Because, said Harlan, your heart doesn't care about anything but what it cares about. That's true, said Blurtso, when I was in love with Beatrice I would have done anything and gone anywhere to be with her. You'll love again, said Harlan. Do you think? said Blurtso. Sure, said Harlan. What if I've become so attached to my routine that I can't change? Then you'll be like the mass of humanity, said Harlan. The mass of humanity? Yes, said Harlan, living lives of quiet desperation. That's sad, said Blurtso. Yes it is, said Harlan. Does the mass of humanity ever follow its heart? said Blurtso. Yes, said Harlan, vicariously, when they read a book or watch a movie. A movie? said Blurtso. Yes, said Harlan, about someone who's following their heart.

40

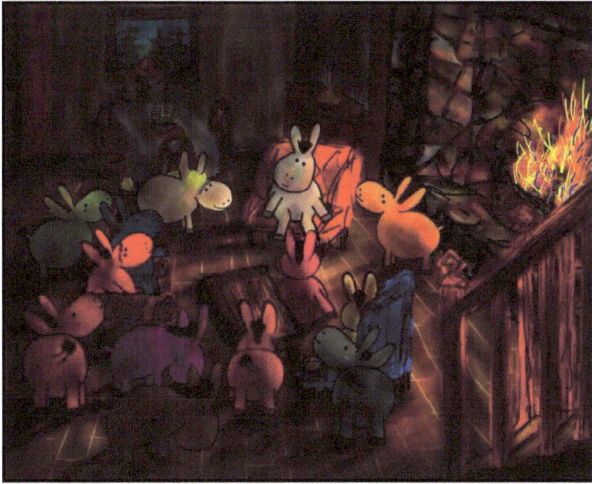

And they said, "Speak to us of beauty,"
and Blurtso replied:
"The horizon is red, and night is falling."

And they said, "Speak to us of aging,"
and Blurtso replied:
"Aging… can speak for itself."

And they said, "Speak to us of invulnerability,"
and Blurtso replied:
"I cannot speak of invulnerability
until you forsake all you desire."

And they said, "Speak to us of intoxication,"
and Blurtso replied:
"What is there inside yourself you need to kill?"

And they gathered and made no sound…
"It is time," said Blurtso, "for pumpkin pie."

I didn't know you were Irish, said Pablo. Actually, said Bonny, I'm Irish, Scottish, Welsh, and English. My oldest ancestors arrived in the Isles around 400 B.C. and lived in all the various regions. I used to celebrate Saint Andrew's Day on November 30th, Saint David's Day on March 1st, and Saint George's Day on April 23rd, but now I celebrate them all on Saint Patrick's Day on March 17th. Does that mean, said Blurtso, you have to drink four times as much beer?

"By yon bonny banks and by yon bonny brays…"

Storm's a brewin'... looks like a nor'easter.
I've always wanted to say that, "looks like a
nor'easter." Every time a breeze blows, someone always says, "looks like a nor'easter." This
is a great place to watch the weather. Maybe I
could get a job on TV? I could start the show
with, "looks like a nor'easter," and then I
could say, "if you don't like the weather, wait
a minute." Wouldn't that be something! To get
paid for saying, "looks like a nor'easter."

Hmm, thought Blurtso, would you look at that... a paperclip. I wonder how it got here? I've never seen Harlan use one, and I don't think *I* ever have. It's got a nice shape. I wonder who made it? Maybe it was a famous artist. I've never seen one in a gallery, so I guess collectors don't call them art. I wonder how they decide? If I made paperclip, I would call it art. It's very symmetrical. And elegant. I wish I had some papers to clip. I suppose I could clip some hay…

Hmmm, thought Blurtso, another paperclip. You go months and months without seeing one, then you see them everywhere you turn. I wonder if they're being discarded as the world goes paperless? And soon they will only be a symbol, an icon for attachments, virtual clips attaching virtual expressions in a virtual world… like so many other forms of attachment.

44

And they said, "Speak to us of quality time,"
and Blurtso replied: "Most of the people
don't spend much time with most of the people
they're around most of the time."

And they said, "Speak to us of busy-ness,"
and Blurtso replied:
"Most people do what they don't need to do
even when they don't need to do it."

And they said, "Speak to us of technology,"
and Blurtso replied: "What does it avail us
to become tools of our tools?"

And they said, "Speak to us of Jacques Derrida,"
and Blurtso replied:
"A koan is an utterance devoid of logic."

And they gathered before the absence of Blurtso
and said, "Speak to us of leadership," and the
absence of Blurtso let the others fill the absence.

45

This is a great bookstore... I wonder why they call it the COOP? Look at all the people downstairs. I've heard almost every language in less than three hours. The world is a very big place, but it's cozy in here. I can smell the rain when the door opens, and feel the breeze. I think I'll have another café mocha before heading home.

Wow, Harvard Square is really crowded! I can't see in any direction. And I can't move. All I can do is stand here. Well... that simplifies things.

Hmm, thought Blurtso, would you look at that…
a crumb. I wonder if it's a bread crumb, or a
cookie crumb, or a graham cracker crumb?
Somehow it escaped its fate. I wonder if it feels
lucky to have been left behind? Or if it misses the
collection of crumbs it came from, and feels sad
for its fortune?

The bathroom at the COOP is always clean,
thought Blurtso, and well-lighted. But there isn't
any music. The light is the most important thing,
of course, and the fact that it's clean. But there
isn't any music.

Final Exam – Greek 201

Name: *Blurtso*

1.) Why did Oedipus kill his father and marry his mother?
Because his friend, Sigmund, told him to.

2.) Who is the goddess Aphrodite?
Aphrodite is the barnyard goddess who visits donkeys in the spring.

3.) What lessons can be learned from the "House of Atreus"?
Don't talk with your mouth full, don't contradict your wife, and always lock the bathroom door.

4.) Why did Zeus become a swan?
Because Leda didn't like woodpeckers.

5.) Why did the Greeks go to war against Troy?
Because Paris stole Helen's pumpkin pie.

6.) How did the Greeks win the battle of Troy?
They built an enormous donkey that scared away all the Trojan horses.

7.) Why was Athena considered the goddess of wisdom?
Because she had grey eyes. Grey is a sign of strength, beauty, and extraordinary intelligence.

8.) Why was Prometheus bound to a rock?
Because trees catch fire.

9.) Who was Homer and what did he write?
Homer was a poet who wrote about a hero named Ysseus who was very odd.

10.) What is a lyre?
A lyre is a string instrument played by Greeks who have lost their trombone.

11.) Explain "hubris":
Hubris is the idea that "pride comes before the fall" —like when you think you're going to get an "A", and you don't.

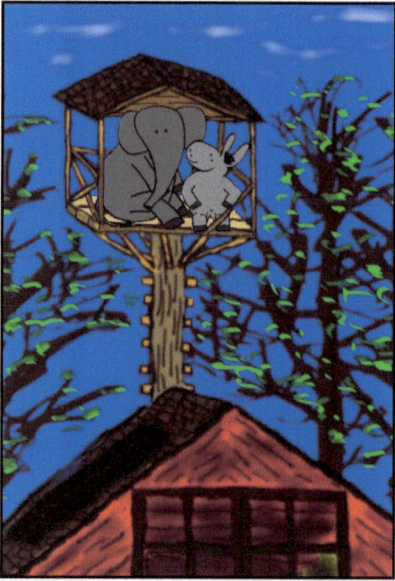

Isn't it amazing, said Blurtso, how people can spend so much time building something, then never look at it when they're done? What do you mean? said Harlan. This treehouse, said Blurtso. Alex and I built it almost two years ago, and when we were building it we selected the boards with the greatest care, then measured and cut them, nailed and braced them, then raised the pole with the house on top, and then we climbed up and never really looked at it again. What's this nick in the rail? said Harlan. That? said Blurtso, that's where I dropped the skill saw when my ice cream fell out of its cone. There's a nail missing here, said Harlan. Yes, said Blurtso, it kept poking out, so I removed it. What are these scratches? That's from my screwdriver, said Blurtso, when I was screwing down the floor boards. And this stain? That's the grape juice I spilled when I was using the nail gun. And this burned spot? That's where I set down the circular sander with the power on. You do beautiful work, said Harlan. Thank you, said Blurtso.

50

What's the matter? said Alex. I'm worried, said Blurtso. Why? said Alex. Because I have to speak at Commencement. But you're not graduating, said Alex. I know, said Blurtso, but my scholarship requires I make an appearance, and the president wants me to give the opening prayer. The opening prayer? said Alex. Yes, said Blurtso, and I don't know what to say. Well, said Alex, you've got to mention god, of course. God? said Blurtso. You mean the great donkey in the sky? Yes, said Alex, and no, because you can't give preference to one god over another. You mean I have to mention *all* the gods? said Blurtso. How do I do that? It's tricky, said Alex. What if I don't mention any? No, said Alex, that won't do…

Let us pray, said Blurtso, Oh god, oh god, oh god, oh god, oh god, oh god, oh god, oh god, oh god, oh god, oh god, oh god, oh god, oh god, oh god, oh god… let's see… where

was I?… oh yes… oh god, oh god, oh god, oh god, oh god, oh god, oh god, oh god, oh god, oh god, oh god, oh god, oh god, oh god, ad Infinitum… amen.

I can hear Harlan downstairs doing the dishes, thought Blurtso. There's something comforting about the clinking of knives and forks and pie tins, after a shared meal, lounging in the lap... of utter satisfaction.

As you circle from side to side, said Blurtso, imagine your arms are a banner attached to a flag pole, a banner waving in a warm breeze, a banner on top of a pumpkin pie factory, announcing a sale on pumpkin pies…

Big Papi, said Harlan, has sure come back strong
from his injury. His injury? said Blurtso. Yes, said
Harlan, his Achilles. His Achilles? said Blurtso, I
thought Achilles was the name of a Greek god. Yes,
said Harlan, a Greek warrior, but it's also the name
of the tendon that connects the heel to the calf. Are
there other parts of the body, said Blurtso, named
after people? There's the Adam's apple, said Harlan.

Why does he grab his Hercules before every pitch?

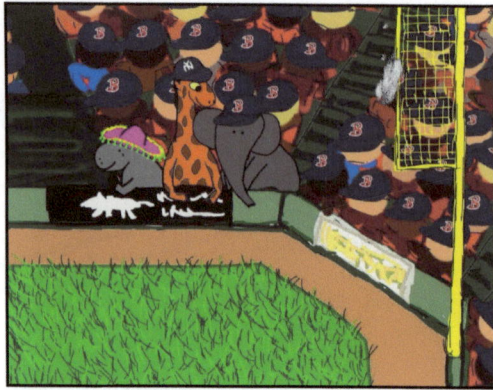

We should play stickball tomorrow, said Alex.
Stickball? said Blurtso. Stickball, said Harlan, is the
street version of baseball. Yes, said Alex, some of
the greatest players in history played stickball…
they say Willie Mays was a 4-sewer hitter. A
4-sewer hitter? said Blurtso. Yes, said Alex, he
could hit the ball four sewer manholes from the
plate. Really? said Blurtso. Yes, said Alex. That's
remarkable, said Blurtso. What's a manhole?

CRACK!

Great work! said Alex. We're 9-2.
Only a game out of first!

What are you doing? said Pablo. I'm hitting Ditto some grounders... he wants to become the next Dustin Pedroia.

No, said Bonny, I didn't know Dustin Pedroia won the gold glove last year. Really? Forty-two doubles and seventeen stolen bases? And eighty-four RBI's? That's a lot for a secondbaseman... No, I don't think you're taller than he is.

Game seven, bottom of the ninth, score tied, two outs, bases loaded… "Ditto" Pedroia steps to the plate… here's the pitch…

Game seven, bottom of the ninth, three balls, two strikes, two outs, runners on first and second... Red Sox up by a run... runners are off with the pitch... it's a slow roller to Dustin "Ditto" Pedroia...

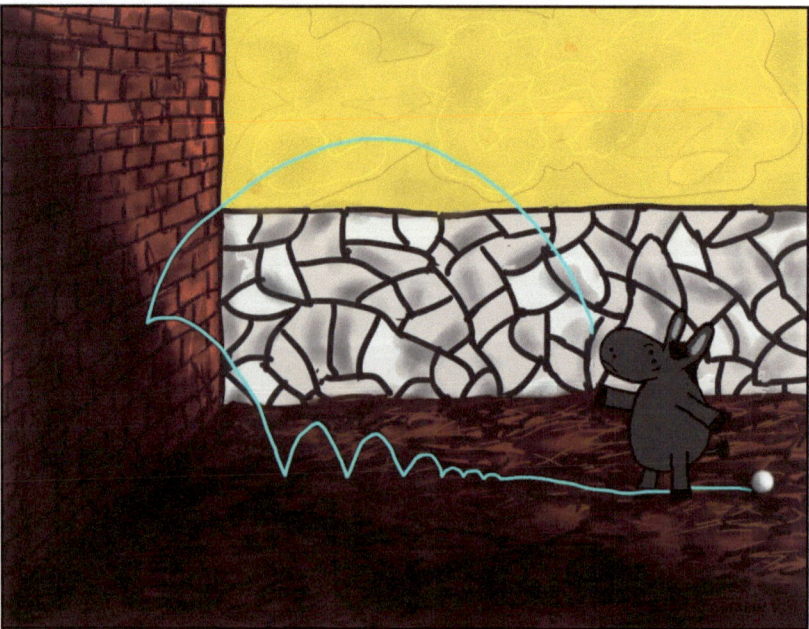

Wow, thought Blurtso, today's game decides the championship. I've never been a champion. I set a record in the ski jump, but was disqualified for being a donkey. That was a relief, because the

paparazzi went away. I don't see any paparazzi here. Or any fans. I guess they're all at home, listening on the radio. I wonder who's doing the broadcast? I'll bet it's Jerry Remy. I wonder if Jerry played stickball? He grew up in Somerset, so he probably played baseball, on real grass. That would be distracting, playing on grass. As distracting as playing in a pumpkin pie factory. You don't see many sporting events in pie factories, for just that reason. I wonder if the winners get a trophy? I'd love to have a trophy, tall and shiny, with an action figure on top. Maybe a donkey taking a Ruthian swing, or a donkey making an over-the-shoulder catch, or a donkey gunning down a runner from third. A trophy would look great in the barn, with some straw around the base. I wonder if being a champion would go to my head? I wonder if I'd begin to stay out late, and go to nightclubs, and get in trouble with the law? The paparazzi would revel in my fall, encouraging the

cracks in my character. And I have many cracks.
I'm not a role model. I have too many vices,
like pumpkin pie, hot cocoa, whipped cream. I
wouldn't want anyone to imitate me. I would be a
terrible champion. But I sure would like a trophy,
tall and shiny, in the middle of the barn.

I forgot to water my pumpkins, thought Pablo,
I wonder what the temperature is today?

I wonder, thought Ditto, if Dustin Pedroia ever
played rightfield?

The zoo is open until dusk, thought Harlan, and
the elephant cage is right by the entrance.

Tomorrow is Ditto's birthday, thought Bonny,
I hope the Dustin Pedroia jersey isn't too small.

The team is really focused today, thought Alex,
the championship is as good as won.

Two outs, bottom of the ninth, one strike from the
championship… here's the pitch… a swing… it's a
long flyball… the centerfielder leaps… she's got
it!… no… she drops it!… it's headed to rightfield…

....

The rightfielder has it!... no... he drops it!...
but here comes the centerfielder!...

Break out the whipped cream and pumpkin pies!

We made a clean sweep of the awards, said Pablo.
Harlan won the homerun title, Alex won the
golden hoof award, Bonny led the league in wins,
I had the highest batting average, and Ditto led the
league in bases on balls. What did I lead in? said
Blurtso. Hitting into double plays, said Alex.

64

What's this? said Blurtso. It's the Baseball Encyclopedia, said Alex, the complete statistical record of every man to ever play Major League Baseball. Wow, said Blurtso, it's like a history book written with numbers instead of letters. Exactly, said Alex. Who is the greatest player of all time? said Blurtso. Babe Ruth, said Alex. Or Ted Williams, said Harlan. Which one is it? said Blurtso. Babe Ruth, said Alex, hit 714 homeruns, a record which lasted for forty years. Yes, said Harlan, but Ted Williams hit 521 homeruns, and he missed five seasons due to military service. So? said Alex. If he had played those years, said Harlan, and averaged 36 homeruns per year, which is what he averaged for his career, he would have hit 700 homeruns as well. Who had the higher batting average? said Blurtso. Babe Ruth batted .342, said Alex. Ted Williams batted .344, said Harlan. Who was a better defensive player? said Blurtso. Babe Ruth, said Alex, until he got fat. Has anyone else hit 700 homeruns? said Blurtso. Yes, said Alex, Barry Bonds and Hank Aaron. Willie Mays hit 660, said Harlan, and he missed two years in the military, so he would have hit 700. Who is the best defensive player in that group? said Blurtso. Willie Mays, said Alex, but

Barry Bonds was also exceptional. Better than Babe Ruth? said Blurtso. Much better, said Harlan. Then why, said Blurtso, isn't Barry Bonds the greatest ever? Because, said Alex, he played in the steroids era. Who was the best all-around player, offense and defense? said Blurtso. Probably Willie Mays, said Alex. Or Barry Bonds, said Harlan. But Babe Ruth, said Alex, is the greatest player of all time. Or Ted Williams, said Harlan.

Hey, a dating site! Maybe I should fill out a profile.

Name: Blurtso
Age: I don't know, I've never cut myself in half to count the rings
Height: I'm not as tall as I think I am
Weight: That's not polite
Self summary: I'm a circumferenceless sphere

I'm good at: Filling out profile questionnaires

The first thing that others notice about me: That I accidentally stepped on their foot

Favorite books, movies, shows, music, food:

books: Remembrance of Pies Past (Marcel Proust), A clean, well-lighted bakery (Hemingway), Where is Ralph Waldo? (Emerson), What's that in the Attic? (Emily Dickenson), Donkey Hotey (Cervantes), The Idiot's Guide to Animal Husbandry

music: You can't roller skate in a buffalo herd (Roger Miller), L'apres midi d'une Trombone (Debussy), Bach's concerto for trombone and cymbal in C flat minor seventh, Beethoven's Moonlight Sonata for Seventy-Six Trombones

movies and shows: Babbling Brook (ambient dvd), Ocean Waves (ambient dvd), Mountain Majesty (ambient dvd), The Jerry Remy Postgame Show

food: organic, sustainably grown, local, free-range, alfalfa-fed pumpkins (from Pablo's garden)

I spend a lot of time thinking about:
Thermonuclear physics, string theory, the event horizon, if Pluto is a planet, how many angels can fit on the head of a donkey, what that smell is

On a typical Friday night I am:
Wondering what night of the week it is

You should message me if: You need an empty pie tin, you found my wristwatch, you lost your Wi-Fi connection, you have an extra pumpkin pie

It only takes two for true love…
I'm half-way there!

****

Curse these clumsy hoofs! said Blurtso. How am I going to update my blog if the only letters I can type are big and fat and round?...

...hddp:// ...bdupdo.pom ...bbossddpdppo.dom ...buugdo.cccob ...booppsdpo.bob ...blllloppdddsss spo.cog ...bplurpppsdso.blob ...booddbppbb...

Hmm… I guess bucket lists are only for people who aren't already doing what they want to do.

Have you ever played chess? said Alex. No, said Blurtso, I don't even know the pieces. That's alright, said Alex, I can teach you… this is the king, and the queen, and the bishop, and the horse, and the castle. Oh said Blurtso, and the little ones are the donkeys?

"A horse is a horse, of course of course, and this one will talk 'til his voice is hoarse. You've never heard of a talking horse? Well, listen to Mister Ed."

I sure would like to meet Mister Ed. Maybe I should take a trip to Hollywood.

Wow! thought Blurtso, Los Angeles! I can hardly wait to see Mister Ed! I wonder where he is? Let's see… the sun is setting, so I think I'll try Sunset Boulevard. And off he went, up and down the street, clippety cloppeting, cloppety clippeting, forth and back and back and forth, looking for Mister Ed. I'm tired, said Blurtso, after several

hours of searching. I think I'll take a nap. Hello, said a policeman. Hello, said Blurtso. May I ask what you're doing? I'm napping on the grass, said Blurtso. It's against the law to nap on the grass. Really? said Blurtso. Yes, said the officer. O.k., said Blurtso, I'll find another place. And off he went, up and down the street, clippety clopping, cloppety clipping, forth and back and back and forth, looking for a new place to nap. Eventually he returned to where he started. Hmmm, he thought, watching the cars arrive, park, and drive away… I know what I'll do! I'll nap in the street! And when the next parking space opened, Blurtso grabbed it. Ahh, that's just perfect, he thought, resting his street-heavy hooves. Hello, said the policeman. Hello, said Blurtso. May I ask what you're doing? I'm napping

in my parking space, said Blurtso. Your parking space? said the officer. Yes, said Blurtso. But you haven't put any money in the meter. Money? said Blurtso. Yes, said the officer, two dollars per hour per vehicle. Am I a

71

vehicle? said Blurtso. No, said the officer, I suppose not. So I can stay? said Blurtso. Yes, said the officer, I suppose so. Thank you, said Blurtso. You're welcome, said the officer. And so it was, after four days on the train and another day in the hills of Hollywood, that Blurtso lay down in his parking space and slipped, as the sun set on West Sunset Boulevard, into a deep and dreamless sleep.

Ahhhh, thought Blurtso, drinking the water the sprinklers had left in the gutter. What a lovely morning! Let's see… what shall I have for breakfast? The grass looks tasty. Mmmm, juicy and fresh, and a little bit spicy! Hello officer, said Blurtso when his friend walked by. Hello Blurtso, said the policeman. Have a nice day! said Blurtso. You too! said the officer. And as the day passed, Blurtso became more and more enamored of his space, chatting with the people, watching the cars, and enjoying the grass beneath his nose. This place has everything! thought Blurtso, settling down for the night. Fresh water, green grass, friendly people… and warm pavement to sleep on. No wonder people love California!

I wonder if I should search for Mr. Ed? thought Blurtso. Where would I look? Sooner or later he's bound to come by here. Maybe I should plant a garden? The grass is really growing with the additional fertilizer. What should I plant? I'll plant pumpkins, of course, and carrots, tomatoes, and corn… and maybe an apple tree. Yes, an apple tree would be splendid. I wonder what Mister Ed grows in his garden? I'm sorry, said the policeman, but the city has made a ruling on your case. My case? said Blurtso. Yes, said the policeman. The

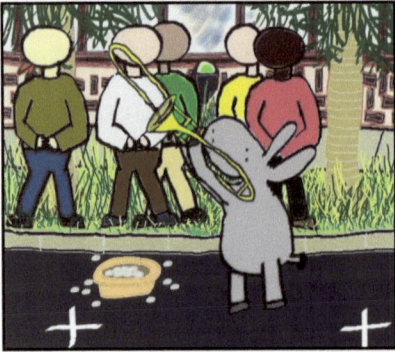

city has decided you've got to put coins in the meter. Coins? How am I going to get coins?

Hello chicken, said Blurtso. Where did you come from? You need a place to stay? Of course you can stay. My parking space is your parking space.

Goodness me! Look at all these chickens!

And the people gathered before him and said, "Blurtso of the sacred space, teach us." And Blurtso replied, "Teach us?" And the people echoed, "Teach us." And Blurtso replied, "Teach what?" And the people explained, "We do not love all who are among us. We do not love all others. And we are ashamed." And Blurtso replied, "What will thou doest when thou seest a tempest in the offing?" And the people replied, "We shall seek shelter." And Blurtso said, "And what will thou doest when thou encounterest danger in thine path?" And the people replied, "We shall pursue a new path." And Blurtso said, "And what will thou doest when thine well of poison smellest?" And the people replied, "Drink we shall not." And Blurtso said, "Just as with nature thou wouldst, so with one another thou shouldst. For each one of thou, in beingst thineself, is for some other a storm, a danger, or a poison. And another for thou shallst be these same things too. So feelest not ashamedst that thou revelst not in the company of all, but rather recognizest the right to existest of the poison, the danger, and the storm, and rejoicest in the natural wisdom that wouldst lead thou unto safety and keepest thou from harm."

It's not easy being a modern-day Messiah.

Wow! thought Blurtso. California sure got
crowded! Maybe I should go for a walk...

Ahhh, thought Blurtso, it's good to be walking,
one hoof after another,
with no place to go, moving down the road...

As Blurtso made his way across the land, he paused to consider the travelers who had made the journey before him… the young ones with innocence in their eyes, in search of adventure; the middle-aged ones, discouraged but not defeated, far from family and in search of a job; and the old ones, irretrievably detached and free from the weight of hopefulness, blown from town to town like leaves on the wind. At night, drawn by the glow of a flame, they would gather in silence, reflecting on the trials behind and the trials ahead, until one, reaching into his pocket, would pull out an harmonica, wipe it on his sleeve, and softly begin to play…

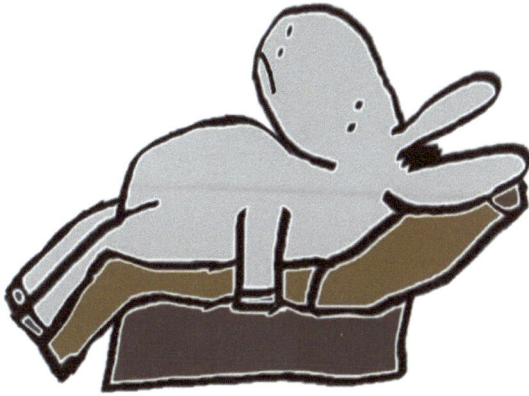

Well then, said the psychiatrist, what seems to be
the problem? I can't find Mister Ed, said Blurtso.
Mister Ed? said the psychiatrist. The talking horse,
said Blurtso. I see, said the psychiatrist, and how
long have you been looking for him? I went all the
way to California and back, said Blurtso, and he
was nowhere to be found, though I did meet
Rocinazo. Rocinazo? said the psychiatrist. Yes,
said Blurtso, a distant relative of Don Quijote's
horse, Rocinante. I see, said the psychiatrist, and
did you meet any other horses? Well, said Blurtso,
I looked for Little Joe's horse, Cochise, on the
Ponderosa, but I couldn't find him. And I would
have liked to meet Zorro's horse, Tornado, and of
course the Lone Ranger's horse, Silver, but most
of all I wanted to meet Mister Ed. I see, said the
psychiatrist. I think I can make a diagnosis. Really?
said Blurtso. Yes, said the psychiatrist, I'm afraid
you have a case of "horse envy."

I'm depressed, said Blurtso. Depressed? said Pablo.
Yes, said Blurtso, I went all the way to California
and I didn't find Mister Ed. Mr. Ed? said Pablo.
The talking horse, said Blurtso. Oh, said Pablo, the
great white whale. What? said Blurtso. The great
white whale, said Pablo, the agonizing obsession,
Moby Dick, the one thing you cannot have, the
thing that takes over your life until all your pas-
times and pleasures lose their appeal. Yes, said
Blurtso, that's it... even the last pumpkin pie I
ate... well... it tasted like a head of lettuce. Yes,
said Pablo, the agonizing obsession. What can I do?
said Blurtso. The thing to do, said Pablo, is not to
focus on the object of the obsession, but on the
process. The process? said Blurtso. Yes, said Pablo.
You went to California. You must have discovered
some things along the way. Oh yes, said Blurtso, I
saw many marvelous sights, and I met many
animals and people. Well then, said Pablo, those
are the fruits of your obsession. Yes, said Blurtso, it
was a great trip... you know... I feel better already.
So do I, said Pablo. I'm hungry, said Blurtso, let's
have a pumpkin pie!

80

Hmm, I never noticed that before…
now I'll never not notice it again.

"Stay tuned for the News Hour and tonight's
roundtable debate, 'Can black and white be
considered colors, and if so, which one is more
colorful?' moderated by Dr. Jonathan Wellborn
Truington III, renowned taxidermist and Pulitzer
prize-winning author of, *Is White White or is White
the New Black?*"... I think humans, said Blurtso, take
themselves too seriously.

Harlan? said Blurtso. Yes? said Harlan. Are you awake? Yes, said Harlan. What are you thinking of? Einstein's theory of time, said Harlan. What? said Blurtso. You know, said Harlan, the discovery that time passes more slowly the faster you move. Is that true? said Blurtso. Yes, said Harlan. So I would live longer, said Blurtso, if I moved more quickly? Yes, said Harlan. And if I ran in my sleep, said Blurtso, I would get more sleep?

****

Harlan? said Blurtso. Yes? said Harlan. Are you awake? Yes, said Harlan. What are you thinking about? Mortality, said Harlan. Mortality? said Blurtso. Yes, said Harlan, do you believe in reincarnation? I'm not sure, said Blurtso, what's re-incarnation? That's when your soul comes back as a different animal. After you die? said Blurtso. Yes, said Harlan, if you live a good life you come back as a higher one, and if you live a bad life you come back as a lower one. A lower animal? said Blurtso. Yes, said Harlan. Like a human? said Blurtso.

****

Harlan? said Blurtso. Yes? said Harlan. Are you awake? Yes, said Harlan. What are you thinking about? said Blurtso. Differences, said Harlan. Differences? said Blurtso. Yes, said Harlan, political, religious, and personal differences. Like what one person thinks is fun and another does not, and what one thinks is proper and another does not, and what one thinks is necessary and another does not. Yes, said Blurtso, it's amazing we ever get along. I suppose, said Harlan, that's what love is for.

****

Harlan? said Blurtso. Yes? said Harlan. Are you awake? said Blurtso. Yes, said Harlan. Have you ever thought about suicide? said Blurtso. Yes, said Harlan. Why do you think people do it? I don't know, said Harlan, I suppose we all need at least one reason, one pure activity to go on living. One activity? said Blurtso. Yes, said Harlan. Like what? said Blurtso. Like anything, said Harlan, love is an activity.

Harlan? said Blurtso. Yes? said Harlan. Do you
ever get frightened? Frightened? said Harlan. Yes,
said Blurtso. About what? said Harlan. About
things, said Blurtso. Things? said Harlan. Yes,
said Blurtso, things in general. Of course, said
Harlan. Really? said Blurtso. Sure, said Harlan.
Why do you suppose that is? Well, said Harlan,
when you consider how fragile things are, things
like life and love and happiness, and how they're
certain to vanish tomorrow, and the nothingness
that follows, it's natural to be frightened. Yes it is,
said Blurtso. But there's room for optimism, said
Harlan. There is? said Blurtso. Sure, said Harlan,
we still have a quarter tin of hot chocolate
powder, and an entire can of whipped cream.

****

Harlan? said Blurtso. Yes? said Harlan.
Are you awake?
Yes, said Harlan. Good, said Blurtso.

Harlan? said Blurtso. Yes? said Harlan. Do you think anyone else stays awake like we do, talking in the dark? Yes, said Harlan, I'm sure they do. What do you think they say? said Blurtso. They tell tales, said Harlan, of what they did during the day, or say silly things like children who can't sleep, or say sad things about the sorrows they hope to change, and then they sing lullabies to each other, until they forget their sorrows, and sleep like children who *can* sleep.

****

Harlan? said Blurtso. Yes? said Harlan.
Will you sing me a lullaby?

****

Harlan? said Blurtso. Yes? said Harlan. Why are elephants afraid of mice? We're not afraid, said Harlan, we just don't like to step on them. Oh, said Blurtso. There's nothing that breaks an elephant's heart, said Harlan, like stepping on a mouse. Elephants are very sensitive, said Blurtso. Yes, said Harlan, we are.

****

Harlan? said Blurtso. Yes? said Harlan.
I'm glad you're so sensitive.

Hmm, thought Blurtso, a dead bird. You don't see many dead birds. I wonder why not? With so many birds in the trees you'd expect the ground to be covered with them, like leaves in autumn.

Why do humans, said Blurtso, interfere with nature? Humans, said Pablo, are creatures of nature, and as creatures of nature they inevitably act naturally, so their conscious interference in nature must be working in the interests of nature, even if that interference turns out to be nature's way of eliminating humans.

Is it possible, said Virginia, to become a sound?
What? said Ditto. I was lost in the melody
of your voice.

It's good for trees to have deep roots, said Ditto.
And for the soil, said Virginia, to have tall trees.

What am I doing? Nobody wants me here, and even if I convince them to want me, I don't want me here. Remarkable, what an ass will do.

What a nice barn… I wonder where the animals are? And the people? It's hard to believe they have abandoned this barn. I guess they've all rushed off to the future.

"Blurtso sits on the fence"

Hmm, the grass is equally green.

It's easy to identify problems from up here,
but impossible to do anything.

I thought this would be more comfortable.

Look at the people on both sides
working furiously to fortify the fence,
as if life depended on it.

I'm several feet off the ground,
but I don't feel courageous.

Hey… is that Robert Frost?

I wish I could remember, said Blurtso, trying to remember what it was he wanted to remember. It must be here somewhere, in my brain, ears, eyes, hoofs, or smell. It must be something important. Blurtso looked at the grass in front of his nose and took a bite. Mmmm, he thought, remembering how good grass tastes in the early morning on a spring day. Mmmm, he thought, taking another bite and forgetting that he was trying to remember. Now I remember! he said, running off to meet the others who had remembered to remember.

Forget it, said Blurtso, trying not to remember. He looked at the grass in front of his nose and took a bite. Mmmmm, he thought, remembering how good grass tastes and forgetting what he didn't want to remember.

90

Satisfaction is what you recognize
when you emerge from total engagement
in a passionate endeavor…

Hey… absinthe improves your aim.

Some people say these woods are haunted, said
Pablo, they say the shadows of the trees are spirits
longing to break free. I don't think my shadow
longs to break free, said Blurtso, I think it would
be lonely without me.

It occurred to me today, said Bonny, that everything in the universe can be described by a single
word. What? said Pablo. Yes, said Bonny, all the
diversity, all the different perspectives, the different realities that people believe in. What word is
that? said Pablo. The word "or," said Bonny. Or?
said Pablo. Yes, said Bonny. I don't understand,
said Pablo. Well, said Bonny, do you agree that
existence is based on perception? Perception? said
Pablo. Yes, said Bonny, that everything that exists
is a relationship, that is, everything I hear, touch,
taste, and smell is some kind of vibration interact-
ing with my brain, which translates that vibration
into what I know as light, color, sound, and smell.
And without that relationship those vibrations
would be no more than "one hand clapping". Yes,
said Pablo, I believe that's true. So apart from my
brain, said Bonny, or some type of brain, the world
is devoid of light, heat, weight, motion, space, and
time, because, like a current that won't flow
through a wire until the positive pole is connected

with the negative, the vibrations of light and heat do not become light or heat until they have a point of arrival, until they interact with some type of organism. Yes, said Pablo. And because they interact differently with different organisms—the bumble bee's perception of light is not the same as the donkey's, or the human's, the dog "hears" vibrations that donkeys and humans cannot, and though all donkeys are born with similar organs, some hear better or see better or smell better than others—the experience of "reality" is different for all living things. Yes, said Pablo, I believe that. So if someone asked you, said Bonny, to define reality, you would have to say that reality is this "or" that "or" that "or" that, depending on who is experiencing it and how they are experiencing it. Yes, said Pablo. Well, said Bonny, that is the philosophy of "or". I like it, said Pablo, the universe reduced to a word. Too bad, said Bonny, it can't be reduced to a letter. It can, said Pablo. It can? said Bonny. Sure, said Pablo, the Spanish word for "or" is "o". O? said Bonny. Yes, said Pablo. That's wonderful, said Bonny, a perfect circle, except…Except what? said Pablo. Our circle is incomplete, said Bonny. Why? said Pablo. Because, said Bonny, the universe consists of all the perceptions of all the organisms, so it is not only this "or" that, but this "and" that, "and" that "and" that "and" that. Yes, said Pablo. So a better philosophy, said Bonny, would be the philosophy of "and". Yes, said Pablo, and "and" is still a single word. Too bad, said Bonny, it can't be reduced to a letter. It can, said Pablo. It can? said Bonny. Sure, said Pablo, the Spanish word for "and" is "y". Y? said Bonny. Yes, said Pablo. Well, said Bonny, "y" isn't a perfect circle, but it looks like two rivers flowing into one… diversity flowing into unity. Yes it does, said Pablo. Of course, said Bonny, by its very nature "and" would have to include "or"… so the ultimate philosophy would have to be a combination of "and" and "or". You're right, said Pablo, and "y" and "o" make "yo" which is Spanish for "I". I? said Bonny. Yes, said Pablo. That's wonderful, said Bonny. Why? said Pablo. Because, said Bonny, it brings us back to

where we started, to reality created by individual perception, except that this new "I" or "yo" is not the individual, separate "I" that we started

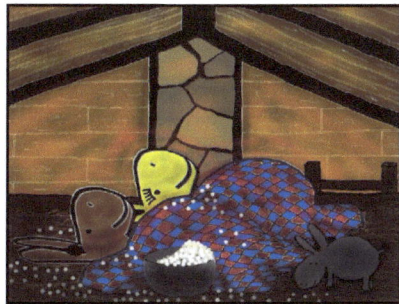

with, but a comprehensive "I", a "yo" composed of all the perceptions of all the organisms from all perspectives. That *is* wonderful, said Pablo. Yes it is, said Bonny. You're very profound, said Pablo. Thank you, said Bonny, is there any more popcorn?

I don't think I'm very human, said Blurtso. Why
not? said Harlan. I've been watching television
all day, said Blurtso, and I haven't seen a single
thing I liked. What do you mean? said Harlan.
Well, said Blurtso, I'm not interested in owning an
automobile, I don't want insurance, I don't eat
meat, I don't drink beer, I don't care about celebri-
ties, I'm not in a hurry, and I'd rather play a sport
than watch it. Well, said Harlan, that just about
covers it. And oh yes, said Blurtso, I have no
interest in movies where things are blowing up.
You're right, said Harlan, you're not very human.
What do you think it would be like, said Harlan, if
there were more donkeys on TV? I don't really
know, said Blurtso, I guess there would be a lot
more wandering around… sort of like a golf tour-
nament without balls and clubs.

Hmm, thought Blurtso, number 82. Everywhere I go, someone is always giving me a number. And it's different every time. I'm starting to think they don't know who I am.

Hmm, thought Blurtso, number 67. There are 53 numbers in front of me. I wish those numbers didn't exist, except that they refer to people... which is easy to forget.

Hmmm… it sure is nice to swing back and forth… and synchronize your breath to the motion… inhale forward, exhale back, inhale forward, exhale back… Hmmm… I'm really soaring… wow, I guess it's as close as I'll get to flying… unless I go para-sailing… like Pablo in Mexico… Pablo doesn't have a timid bone in his body… maybe I should write a famous novel and make Pablo the hero… but then my novel would be fact instead of fiction… and I already have enough facts in my life… like the fact I'm late for school… Hmmm… it sure is relaxing… to synchronize your breath… I wonder if the birds synchronize their breath to the beat of their wings… it would be nice to be able to fly, but I wouldn't want to be a bird… wings are even clumsier than hooves… especially for cell phones and texting… I don't think I've ever seen a bird texting… no matter how nervous he was… and birds are very nervous… I guess I would be too, if I were smaller than a cat… but I'm bigger than cats… and that simplifies things… like swinging… back and forth… and in and out… I wonder if my class is over… I wonder if I missed the final… I think today was the last day… Hmmm… it sure is relaxing… to swing back and forth… and breathe in and out… I'll bet I could swing all day… if I didn't get hungry… I'll bet I could just keep on swinging… back and forth, and in and out… marking my path… as effortlessly as… the path... of a planet.

I admire grass, thought Blurtso. It never gets discouraged. It keeps on growing no matter how often they mow it down. And in a storm it just bends in the wind. It makes me happy to think… we are what we eat.

Do you miss living on the Common? said Blurtso.
Yes and no, said Harlan, I've never been happier
than I am sharing your barn, but there's always
something lost whenever there's something gained.

Hmm, thought Blurtso, would you look at that, the
first snow before the leaves are down. I suppose
we're not always ready... for what the world brings.

100

www.ingramcontent.com/pod-product-compliance
Lightning Source LLC
Chambersburg PA
CBHW051238090426
42742CB00001B/5